NUMEROLOGY
FOR YOUR HOME
Using Abundance Codes to Shift Your Life

Printed in the United States of America

Spellbound Publishers, 2018

ISBN 978-0-9977349-7-3
PCN 2018951141

NUMEROLOGY
FOR YOUR HOME
Using Abundance Codes to Shift Your Life

By Amanda Rieger Green, MPH

Spellbound
PUBLISHERS

PRAISE FOR NUMEROLOGY
FOR YOUR HOME

"This is a terrific contribution toward more aware, enlightened living. And Amanda writes intentions better than anybody, anywhere. They're works of art."

-*Terry Hobbs Heller, PhD*

"As a novice to the power of "numbers" and a believer in Amanda's abilities, I took her advice blindly and changed the numerological energy of my house by placing a #7 in my doorway. Transparently, I had no expectations and went on with my life routine as usual.

"What I experienced was transformational yet subtle. My personal energy went from a place of feeling stuck and lethargic to motivated and ready to improve my life in a holistic way. My home became a haven where I could commit to a daily routine of meditation, reading, writing, affirmations, visualizations and working out for 30 minutes in the morning.

"I have posted my morning affirmations in the bathroom next to my mirror and honestly can say that I believe that every day has the opportunity to be the best day of my life. Over the last three months I have lost weight, shifted my abilities to self-love, and given more of myself in an organic way to the rest of the world. This exponential growth and new found energy has also attracted a good friend and neighbor to assist me in creating a year-long master plan for all important aspects of my life. I am now able to evaluate current challenges, wins, and come up with a specific action plan to attack all of the weakness and pain points I currently have.

"There is nothing like having the correct tools to take you where you want to go and creating a mindset that gives you the confidence to manifest your dreams. I am just getting started but I have never been this truly happy and motivated to offer the best version of myself to the world. I can't wait to see what other doors open as I continue to lean into this energy shift and self-development journey. I am a believer!"

-Katie Shannon, Brand and Marketing Strategist

I dedicate this fun spiritual tool-kit to my mother Lisa, who believes in and supports me no matter what! 'Grateful for you, Momma, in all of our lifetimes together.

It is my intention that I trust my body to put me in the right place at the right time, in line with my Higher Self and for the Greater Good . . . one day at a time.

Amanda Rieger Green, MPH

TABLE OF CONTENTS

"We are all just walking each other home."

-Ram Dass

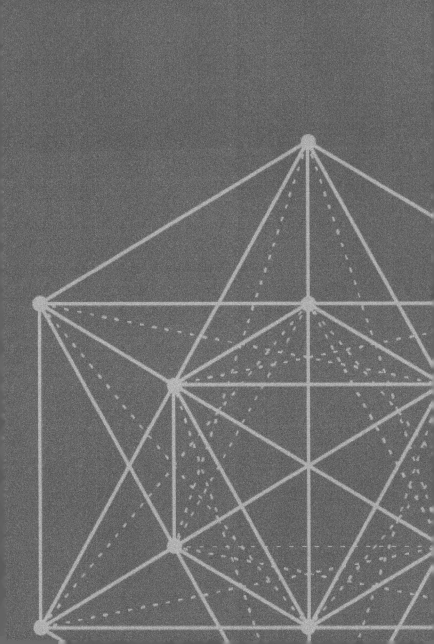

FOREWORD
By Tiffany Harelik, MA

In November of 2016 I called my Dad to discuss whether
or not I should move again. I had moved every year for
several years, and despite my efforts to create a beautiful
space, I still wasn't feeling settled. Dad said, "You need
to make your home a place you run to, not away from."
But I still struggled. No amount of gardening was helping
. . . neither was setting up a pretty meditation corner nor
playing music 'to my house' while I was away. I saged.
I prayed. I looked within. I set New Moon intentions, I
cleared, I worked on myself. But there was still a missing
piece.

Despite my unease, I decided to stay in the house another
year. After all, no matter where you go, there you are.
I decided "I" was the problem—not my house—and I
continued to seek self-development tools and resources.

When I met Amanda she introduced me to address

numerology. My mind was totally blown. If I'm honest, I didn't believe her at first. Could putting a post-it note of a number on my door frame to 'change my address numerology' really work? I was desperate to find that Zen oasis feeling in my home so I was ready to try anything. We calculated the numerology of my address and determined it was a 7. This numerology energy wasn't the greatest fit for my active personality and busy lifestyle given the calm environment I was hoping to create. She suggested we change my address numerology to be a 6 so that I felt more balanced.

I was surprised to find that it only took about two weeks for things to change. Some of the changes weren't comfortable at first, but I was peaceful about what was unfolding because the energy was finally flowing in the right direction. Without hardly any effort on my part, my home felt like the nest I had been yearning to create. I finally had a home that I was running to instead of away from. This is the power of address numerology. This is why I asked Amanda to write this book.

Tiffany Harelik, MA
Wise Skies Astrology
Spellbound Publishers

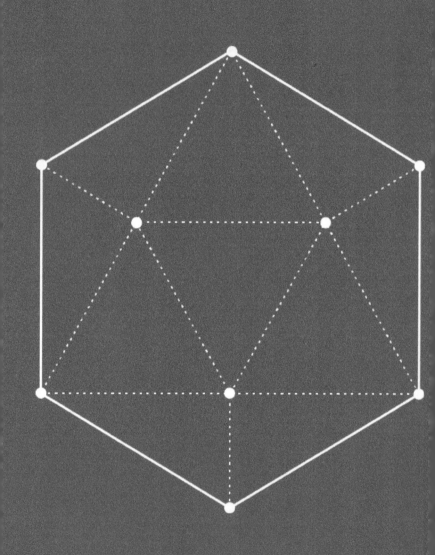

ACKNOWLEDGEMENTS

At the beginning of 2018, I intended to publish a book by the fall. When I send intentions out and believe in them, my next task is to trust Spirit and the magic of divine timing in the orchestration of arranging my vision. Intentions truly are collaborations with destiny. This book is a product of that exciting and frightening process of allowing intentions to unfold. It "fell together" through the collaboration of some wise folks. And for that, I am both in awe and abundantly blessed and grateful.

First, I'd like to gratefully acknowledge Tiffany Harelik and Spellbound Publishers. Tiffany is my co-heart, business partner, dedicated publisher and soul sister. Tiffany, thank you for encouraging me to get this out into the universe, translating concepts and ideas into a simple format for the reader, and keeping me on task. I couldn't ask for a better better partnership or friendship that flows more organically, transparently, and ultimately is bringing one dream to life at a time. Our dynamic-duo is pure abundance!

I'd also like to thank Dr. Terry Heller, aka "Tootie," for totally "getting" the essence of the message of this book and editing it with a believing and honest eye. Her talents and experience as an editor could not have been more in sync with the rhythm and cadence I envisioned creating for the reader. I not only have a trusted editor in her, I have a new friendship and kindred spirit to share this journey of The Abundance Code Series.

Have you seen the cover of this book? I am incredibly thankful for the creative and precise eye of Letitia Smith of White Light Exposure! She is a talented woman whose passion and creative gifts fall in perfect alignment with the book. She brought the design to life with the elements of mystery, sacred geometry, and, of course, the magic of numbers. I'm beyond grateful to have Letitia designing this book series.

Finally, it truly does take a village to raise an author. A huge thank you to my mother, Lisa, for her unwavering support, love, and encouragement of the development of my spiritual gifts. Even through the most trying and fundamentally transformative times she has been my rock and biggest believer. Big love also to family, friends and clients who have trusted me with their Soul Pathology, aligning them with the highest versions of themselves, and for their willingness to contribute to the spiritual awakening on this planet and in the universe. All of these beautiful souls raise my vibration! I am grateful to my "village" for the trust, support and encouragement to "Step Into Your Light & Stand In Your Purpose."

In a conversation a few weeks ago, I asked my husband Dennis what abundance meant to him. True to form, he answered simply by saying abundance means "enough." He has been one of my greatest teachers in tapping into "abundance consciousness" over the last handful of years. I know the vibration of abundance, richness and beauty through you, Dennis. Thank you for your continued support, belief in me, and for always adding to my happiness. I love you.

Last but not least, thank you Tex & Ouisie (my twin labrador retrievers) for generating the vibration of unconditional love over and over again. You ever increase my heartspace.

Introduction

Driving down I-10 between Phoenix and Tucson, Arizona on a business trip in 2007, I was listening to a radio interview with Glynis McCants, "The Numbers Lady." As she talked about numerology, taking calls from listeners and offering insights based on their personal numerology, I suddenly realized that I "knew" the vibrations of numbers. I was actually intuiting what she was going to say, based on the combinations of numbers for each caller. Some people have perfect pitch—I have numbers intuition! I pulled over and just sat there taking it all in. I was stunned. It was as if something had triggered an ancient innate knowledge of numbers—dormant information, stored and un-accessed in my cells and DNA.

There was something else. I also "knew" that there was more to the numbers than their vibrations and characteristics. There were codes. And these codes were coming together for me. I seemed to be able to "crack" them. The show ended, and I finally got back on the road—not quite sure what to do with my new found knowledge of numbers.

It would be years before I would dive deeper into numerology, numbers and codes, and come up with practical applications in my life and the lives of clients— the fruition of the seed that cracked open on the road to Tucson. In the meantime, I learned from great numerology teachers like Hans Decoz and Felicia Bender about vibrations and applications of specific numbers. Their work has supported me and validated information I already "know". . . and has led, ultimately, to my writing this book.

This book is more than a numerology tool for shifting the energy of your environment, it's a code to unlock your super-conscious potential. In these pages you will learn to look at where you are and envision a higher, lighter, easier, in-the-flow version of your life. I'll teach you about aligning with your desires to evoke a life shift that is in line with your life purpose. No small thing, right? Actually, it's all about changing the energy. And that's very doable.

But then, perhaps your life energy is already perfectly aligned—perfect health, relationships, career, home environment, spiritual well-being, abundance as far as the eye can see...your life is beautiful! No? Perhaps things are a little murky here and there? Well, here you go: This book turns on all the lights. It's about helping you with a paradigm shift that enables change, ease, and flow in all areas of your life. Sound impossible? It's not.

The Abundance Codes are tools for expanding your consciousness and for finding the extraordinary in the ordinary. The power we have to become conscious co-creators of our reality is real and attainable. We are already co-creating our reality unconsciously, so why not jump in and do it consciously? Change your numbers, change your life. Sound simple? Well, it is. It's all about energy, vibrations, the stardust we're all made of. You don't have to understand quantum physics to apply the wisdom of the numbers. You can simply use the tools in this book to make it work for you.

The exercises in this book can be mind-blowing. In very little time—a few weeks, a few months—you can change everything, literally. So get started. Take the first step. Decode your life, and then buckle up for a really cosmic ride!

Are you still here? What are you waiting for? Turn the page!

"Whatever we are waiting for

- peace of mind, contentment,

grace, the inner awareness of

simple abundance - it will surely

come to us, but only when we are

ready to receive it with an open

and grateful heart."

-Sarah Ban Breathnach

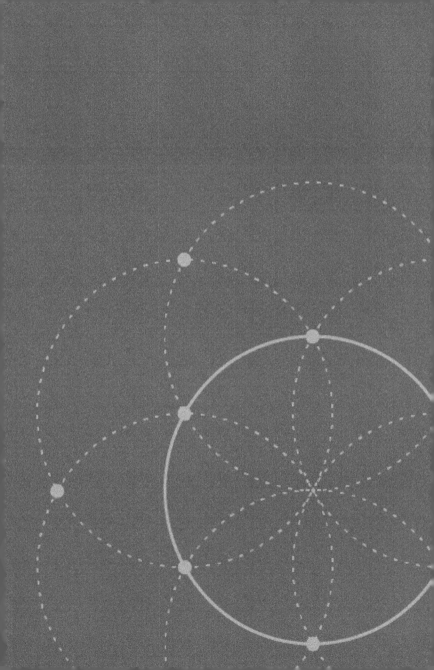

WHAT ARE ABUNDANCE CODES?

CODE: A system of words, letters, figures, or symbols used to represent assigned meanings. —*Merriam Webster Dictionary*

Abundance codes are combinations of numbers and characteristics that symbolize specific vibrational frequencies. These "codes" can reveal your biggest challenges and blocks while simultaneously offering keys for your growth and expansion through meeting those challenges. Abundance codes guide us in understanding how we may be limiting our experience, while also allowing us to tap into something much greater—a way of being more freely engaged in our own human and spiritual existence.

Everything in and around us vibrates at an energetic frequency. Quantum physicists tell us that everything in existence is made up of subatomic particles that are, at their essence, vibrations. From physical matter to emotional states, our entire world and atmosphere can be described in terms of vibrational energy. Different realities have different vibrations which in turn have different identifying frequencies. These frequencies vary in length and tone and make up everything from rocks to thoughts, from peanut butter to skyscrapers. Literally everything is made up of frequencies—including numbers. The numbers you were born with and the numbers that you live with are part of your code.

The Abundance Code Series focuses on ways to understand and change your world for creating more abundance—in health, vitality, emotional well-being, money, relationships . . . every area of your life. In order to experience abundance in all aspects of your life, you need to know the underlying energy patterns you're living with to be able to "crack" your codes. In this book, we focus on the numbers related to your living space.

Numerology is one of the simplest tools to assist you in your abundance code-cracking. By understanding the attributes of the numbers in your address, you can identify how their frequencies support or limit you. Ultimately, learning how to crack your codes helps you to move from a state of lack consciousness into abundance consciousness. You will learn how to create an abundant environment using numbers for your healing and personal development, as well as for fulfillment of your dreams and desires.

Cracking your abundance codes starts with healing false belief systems that no longer serve you. When I began consciously living with more intention, I started recognizing patterns and developing codes that aligned with the energy I wished to generate and attract into my life. I soon recognized I had been living in lack consciousness rather than abundance consciousness since childhood. It was a transformative yet simple connection. It wasn't that I was a pessimist. In fact, I mostly looked for the positive or the good in situations and circumstances. However, at the core of my belief system, I innately believed that I was "less than" or "not enough"—I lived in lack mode! Try this:

Say the word **LACK** aloud.

Now, say the word **ABUNDANCE** aloud.

They sound different. They feel different. In energy terms, "Lack" feels small, short and finite. "Abundance" feels roomy, expansive and infinite. Once I made this connection, I had cracked a code to my Soul Pathology and karmic healing. So, I intentionally released the outdated belief system of my lack consciousness and invited in abundance consciousness.

But, within twenty-four hours, I realized that I needed something more. Simply "intending" to experience and believe in my abundance consciousness was not generating the fundamental "abundant" effect. There were numbers somewhere that needed to be dealt with. Ultimately, as a numerologist, I knew that in order to experience the energy of abundance, I had to crack my own abundance code. And over the next 24 hours, that's exactly what I did. It all started with looking at my personal numerology.

MY PERSONAL NUMEROLOGY: I'M A TRIPLE 9.

When I began unraveling who I was on a soul level, one of the first things I did was decode my personal numerology or, as I refer to it, my "numerology blueprint." My Life Path number is a 9 and my Attitude number is a 9. So, I'm a 99. Funny enough, I was born in a 9 year. So, technically, I'm a 999. I know what you're thinking, because that's what I thought too: "Whoa, that's a lot of 9's!" This simple yet profound code astounded me. It also brought me comfort in knowing that I do have a special blueprint. My numerology, astrology, and all the other fascinating spiritual tools out there make up my unique identifier of who I am—like my thumbprint.

PERSONAL NUMEROLOGY BASICS

In personal numerology, the first two codes to learn are your Life Path number and your Attitude number. While the Life Path number provides information about your role in this lifetime, the Attitude number is a direct reflection of your personality—the way you look at the world—as well as how others perceive you. For those of you into astrology, think of the Life Path number as your Sun sign and the Attitude number as your Rising sign.

LIFE PATH NUMBER = YOUR SOUL PURPOSE.

The Life Path number is the most fundamental part of your numerology blueprint. It is the vibration you arrived with on this earth and in this lifetime, and it's the vibration that you came to master and maneuver. Knowing your Life Path number will help you gain an understanding of how you limit and also free yourself. The Life Path number reflects your behaviors, attitudes, experience, and perspectives in life. It's the first number you want to know and understand. It is like your fingerprint—a number that is uniquely yours.

CALCULATING THE LIFE PATH NUMBER:

Sum up the month you were born + the day you were born + year you were born. Then, reduce it to a single digit number.

Example:

My Birthdate is October 8th, 1980

10-08-1980

$1 + 0 + 0 + 8 + 1 + 9 + 8 + 0 = 27$

Reduce it to a single digit: $2 + 7 = 9$

My Life Path number is a 9.

To learn more about the 9, or your own Life Path number, flip to Chapter 4.

ATTITUDE NUMBER = YOUR ATTITUDE OR PERSONALITY

The Attitude number is exactly what it says it is—your attitude, how other people see or perceive you. It's what you project or how you express yourself to the world around you. I call it an external personification of you.

CALCULATING THE ATTITUDE NUMBER:

Sum up the month you were born + the day you were born. Then, reduce it down to a single digit number, if applicable.

Example:

Again, my birthdate is October 8th.

10-08

$1 + 0 + 0 + 8 = 9$

My Attitude Number is a 9

To learn more about your own Attitude number after you calculate it, jump ahead to Chapter 4.

The Life Path number and the Attitude number are building blocks for your personal numerology blueprint, but there are so many more numbers to explore. You can calculate your Expression or Destiny (the numerology of your name), look into your Soul Urge, your Essence, and so on. Once I knew more about my basic numerology, I began to explore the number codes of my address and how I related to those numbers. That's where I really started applying what I know about the numbers in my personal abundance codes. I decoded the code, so to speak, by putting all it together in one big picture of my life.

While your personal numerology is a fun way to get started in knowing more about yourself, this book is focused on decoding the energy of your home environment. You don't have to know your personal numerology to tap into the magic of your address numerology, but it helps provide more information about you and how you process your world.

Beyond your personal numerology, one of the easiest codes to work with for beginners who want to experience a shift in their lives is through address numerology. Changing the code of your home environment is as simple as putting a post-it note up on your door frame. But you have to know what you're working with before you can determine the code that will be ideal for your shift. In other words: You have to decode to code.

The next chapter gives you a basic understanding of what address numerology is, and how you can work with it, to tap into your own abundance codes. And after you've read this book, you might be interested in other titles in our Abundance Code Series for shifting the energy of your home such as *Astrology for your Home* by Tiffany Harelik, MA.

"Not what we have but what we enjoy, constitutes our abundance."

-Epicurus

WHAT IS ADDRESS NUMEROLOGY?

Have you ever walked in the door of a home or business and just sensed a weird vibe? Whatever it was, you couldn't get comfortable in that space. But there are other places that feel warm and inviting the second you walk in; where you could literally spend hours. Know this: your natural gut instinct is always a step ahead of your rational, reptilian brain. What your intuition tells you is a true picture of what's really "going on" vibrationally.

Every environment vibrates at a different frequency or energy level that is based on the physical address and its numerological code. There are basic energies built into different environments specifically rooted in the numerical vibrations of the address. In other words, each address has a unique energy code. In this book, we refer to this type of code as your address numerology.

Consider your address numerology as the natal chart or "personality" of your address. It's the karmic energy you have to work with. Once you understand the energy inherent in your address numerology, you can work with it, or you can shift it. Using numbers alone, you can create a more compatible environment in order to help you feel more at home in your own living space, or to optimize your goals for the work space in your home.

When we think about address numerology in general, we first consider the "personality" of the address' environment.

- What does the natural environment of the property feel like?

- Does it feel open or closed, cool or warm, friendly or hostile, balanced or out of sync?

- Who spends time here?

- Why did you choose this location?

As a general example of "address personality," let's consider coffee shops. I'm a coffee shop person. I have a couple of go-to coffee shops around town that I spend time in for different reasons. One is my go-to for quality time with friends and the other is where I crank out work and get creatively focused. So my purpose or goal is different for each coffee shop. Not surprisingly, the numerology of these spaces is in line with the personality of the environment and its effectiveness in meeting my personal purpose in those spaces. The one I go to for quality time resonates with a 9 energy ("charisma"), while the one I go to for work is a 6 ("authenticity"). There's a difference. You can feel it.

Keep in mind that numerology for addresses is only one of the factors at play, including how the numbers interact with your own personal numerology. This is why one space may be great for Person A to work in, but not Person B. Regardless of personal numerology, address numerology can give you the basic information on which environment may or may not be conducive to the experience you are looking for. The actual physical address (the numerical part) is the most fundamental element of the energetic frequencies. The address is like the foundation of a house—it's where you start to build.

What I know from personal experience and in working with clients: When you use these simple tricks to change the number codes in your address to be in alignment with your goals and desires (typically a home or business), a gradual shift will occur in attitudes, behaviors, and dynamics within a couple of weeks. Give it a month or so and you can notice a significant transformation within yourself, the space, and anyone spending time there. It's all about the energy.

"What is called genius is the abundance of life and health."

-Henry David Thoreau

CALCULATING YOUR ADDRESS NUMEROLOGY

Anyone can learn how to calculate address numerology by understanding a few basic principles. It's easier than you think!

In analyzing address numerology, both the name of the street and the number can be individually calculated, and each reduced to a single digit (1-9). The name of the street, avenue, boulevard, or other designation is less important because the street name is shared by many other addresses. But the numbers of your address are specifically associated with your exact location, thus having a more personal impact on your energy.

Each of the single digits, the numbers 1 – 9, have various frequencies that translate into character traits. Like any personality there are going to be some ideal qualities and some challenging qualities. Think of it this way: The characteristics of the numbers are similar to the character traits of zodiac signs in astrology. Each sign has both optimal traits and less desirable traits. It's the same with numbers. You'll learn more about these in Chapter 4.

As for zero: Your address may have a 0 in it, but the numerology will not sum up to 0. Therefore, having a 0-home is not possible. When we look at the 0, it's like a quartz crystal: it enhances everything around it. In other words, the 0 magnifies the traits of the numbers it's connected to. This is why we stick with the numbers 1-9 when discussing your address numerology.

Once you look at the numerology of the address (I'll walk you through the calculation below), you can then determine if the vibe is supporting you or limiting you. Is your address numerology facilitating a lack or an abundance consciousness? This is where it gets fun. Now you can decide if the current vibration of your home is conducive to what you want to attract into that environment, and into your life, to make your life more abundant.

Hint: Knowing the personality of your address numerology is the initial step to decoding the energy of your home environment for abundance.

Don't worry, you don't have to move to get a different vibe or turn down the house of your dreams because the numbers don't add up. If you don't feel the address numerology is compatible with your personal aspirations, you can change it! This book has effective tools for changing the numerology of your home address with a few simple steps. And it only takes a few minutes!

THE BASICS

1. Start with the numbers of your address.
2. Add them up.
3. Reduce it all to a single digit.

Simple Numerical Addresses

2705 Canyon Drive

Numbers: 2705

Add them up: $2 + 7 + 0 + 5 = 14$

Reduce it: $1 + 4 = 5$

For this address, the vibration is a 5.

What if I have a "numerical" address with letters in it?

You are probably wondering about the significance of the words and letters in your address. Yes, letters have associated vibrations and characteristics too. This adds another layer to the energy of your environment. The Pythagorean number table for the alphabet is the most commonly used table and it is what we will use for the alphabetical numerology in this book. For calculating the numerology for letters of the alphabet, use the chart below.

Pythagorean Alphabet Numerology Chart

1	2	3	4	5	6	7	8	9
A	B	C	D	E	F	G	H	I
J	K	L	M	N	O	P	Q	R
S	T	U	V	W	X	Y	Z	

Addresses with Letters

2205 Apartment C Canyon Drive

Numerical Portion: 2205

Add it up: $2 + 2 + 0 + 5 = 9$

Apartment: $C = 3$

Notes:
As a rule, we do not include "apartment," "unit," or "building" in the alphabetical calculation.

Use the Pythagorean alphabetical numerology chart to find the numerical association for the letter C.

Sum it up: $9 + 3 = 12$

Reduce it: $1 + 2 = 3$

The address numerology is a 3.

Mixed Addresses (letters & numbers)

3306 Unit E4 Canyon Drive

Numerical Portion: 3306

Add it up: $3 + 3 + 0 + 6 = 12$

Unit: E3

$E = 5$

$5 + 3 = 8$

Add it up: $12 + 8 = 20$

Reduce it: $2 + 0 = 2$

The address numerology is a 2.

Two Numerical Units, Buildings, or Apartments

153 Peace Street, Units 3 & 4

Numerical Portion: 153

$1 + 5 + 3 = 9$

Units: 3 & 4

$3 + 4 = 7$

Sum it up: $9 + 7 = 16$

Reduce it: $1 + 6 = 7$

The address numerology is a 7.

Two Alphabetical Units, Buildings or Apartments

24 Charles Circle Apartment E & F

Numerical Portion: 24
2 + 4 = 6

Apartments E & F

E = 5

F = 6

5 + 6 = 11

Sum it up: 6 + 11 = 17

Reduce it: 1 + 7 = 8

The address numerology is an 8.

"Doing what you love is the cornerstone of having abundance in your life."

-Wayne Dyer

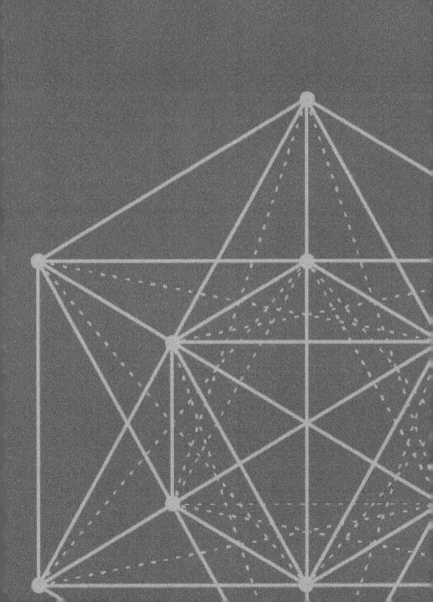

THE TRAITS OF THE NUMBERS: 1-9

#1

Drive • Confidence • Hustle
Independence • Yang • Masculine
Goal-Driven • Organized • Focused

PIONEERS | INVENTORS | LEADERS

*I am open-minded, patient, and tolerant
with myself and those around me.*

LOVE THE ONE YOU'RE WITH

#DoubleOrNothing

Balance • Harmony • Relationships
Feminine • Intuitive • Sensitive
Agreeable • Diplomatic • Flow • Trust

COUPLES | BUSINESS PARTNERSHIPS | TEAMMATES

I set and maintain healthy boundaries in all aspects of my life and relationships.

ATTRACTION RATHER THAN PROMOTION
#Three'sCompany

Creativity • Pizazz • Charisma
Influence • Intuition • Optimism
Wonder • Sass

ENTERTAINERS | ARTISTS | RESTAURANTS

Rest, relaxation, and healthy self-care come naturally to me.

ORGANIZATION STATION

#Get'ErDone

Processes • Order • Tidiness
Consistency • Routine
Organization • Stability • Roots
Foundation • Discipline

BANKS | CPAS | LAW FIRMS

*I am open-minded and willing to
relinquish control, effortlessly allowing
ease and flow into my life.*

LIGHTNING STRIKES TWICE

#ReadySetGo

Adventure • Adrenaline • Freedom
Entertainment • Flexibility
Independence • Momentum • Change
Selfish Action • Dynamic Force

**TRAVELERS | SALESPEOPLE | NEWLY
COMING OUT OF A RELATIONSHIP**

*I am accountable and consistent and easily
create balance in all areas of my life.*

THE NESTER
#HomeIsWhereTheHeartIs

Comfort • Companionship • Nurturing
Nesting • Warm • Loving • Authentic
Connection • Unity • Love
Compassion • Protective

**FAMILIES | NEWLYWEDS | HEALTH
CARE COMMUNITY CENTERS**

*I trust my voice and maintain
interdependence in all relationships
and situations.*

THE PASSIONATE PATH OF PURSUIT
#BloomWhereYourePlanted

Wisdom • Seekers • Philosophers
Quest for Truth • Metaphysics
Heightened Awareness • Knowledge
Analytical • Mystery

**MYSTICS | PROFESSORS | WRITERS |
RESEARCHERS | SCHOOLS**

*Collaboration, connection, and the
sharing of ideas happens organically and
feels enlightening.*

RISK & REWARD
#GoForTheGold

Infinity • Fluidity • Abundance • Power
Prosperity • Initiating • Momentum
Risk and Reward • Expansion

**ENTREPRENEURS | ATHLETES | BROKERS
AND AGENTS**

*I experience peace and serenity in the
present, while creating stability and
consistency.*

THE GREAT CONNECTION
#FullCircle

Experience • Integrity • Innate Wisdom
Connectedness • High Standards
Charisma • Influence • Relatable Familiar

**COMMUNITIES | CLUBS | TEAMS
SUPPORT SERVICES**

*Joy, happiness, and fun are priorities in
my life and allow me to feel free.*

#1 THE BOSS

If your address numerology adds up to 1, get ready for a heavy dose of drive, confidence, hustle, and a strong sense of independence. If you are living in a 1-home, you'll experience the head honcho vibe on a regular basis. The number 1 is literally #1 and likes to be #1. #TheBoss.

The 1-home promotes full-steam-ahead mentality and has an extroverted "yang" drive. You'll have an eye-on-the-prize mentality and be able to put your vision in actionable items. The energy there is linear and is all about achieving goals, accomplishing tasks, and checking boxes off your list.

A 1-home tends to be pioneering, organized, determined, and focused. Because this energy can generate overly driven behaviors and workaholic tendencies, it is wise to incorporate a plan for healthy work/life balance to stabilize the energy.

Watch out: This energy does not "go with the flow"—it does not promote balance, harmony, community or collaboration. A 1-home feels predominantly masculine, and the residents can dominate anything or anyone in order to achieve goals and feel a sense of accomplishment. This dynamic can feel like a horse with blinders, knocking down anything in its path and solely focusing on the individual goal, forgetting that teamwork and collaboration often-times create a more well-rounded vision.

In a 1-home, it is helpful to invite open-mindedness, tolerance for self and others, and serenity in your intentions. After all, what's the point of achieving your goals if they don't fulfill you?

In a 1 space, it is possible to be hyper-focused on the goal and forget to enjoy the journey.

Antidote: Routine gratitude lists are ideal. Volunteer. Find ways to be of service.

Ideal for:
Self-employment
Home-based businesses
Pioneers
Inventors
Motivating behaviors

Unsupportive of:
Newlyweds or couples
Community activity
Yoga & meditation
Charity or church work

Complementary colors:
Red
Yellow
Gold
Black

Crystals that promote grounding, stability, and endurance:
Red Jasper
Rutilated Quartz
Obsidian

Simple tools & tricks for balancing the energy of the 1:
Keep fresh flowers around.
Create a meditation or relaxation space.
Play peaceful music.
Designate a workspace separate from your sleep/resting space.

Home Intention for living in the energy of 1:
My home will feel focused, clear, and express my individuality while creating equal space for rest, rejuvenation, and fulfillment.

Work Intention for home-officing in the energy of 1:
My home-office environment will foster achievement, success, and drive, while organically incorporating balance, open-mindedness, and sustainability.

#2 LOVE THE ONE YOU'RE WITH

If your address numerology adds up to 2, your home is an ideal environment for fostering and nurturing relationships. Your home will feel both agreeable and diplomatic. This energy is all about two sides and is ideal for promoting flow and trust. The 2 is a primarily feminine energy, thus 2-home residents can tap into their intuitive, receptive, and sensitive sides. Living or working in a 2-home encourages balance and harmony, and supports a give-and-take kind of approach to life. #DoubleOrNothing

Think of it this way: it's as simple as 1 + 1 = 2. If you are living in a 2-home, you'll have an opportunity to learn and grow within a relationship. Sometimes this feels like a blessing, and sometimes it feels like a curse. Be aware that if left unbalanced, the 2 energy can feel somewhat manipulative, inflexible, and moody.

Watch out: The vibe in a 2 environment can make you forget where you begin and the other person ends. Codependency and enmeshment is a reality with the low vibes of this energy. The 2 vibe tends to be stubborn, thus the pendulum can swing from fiercely independent to codependent in a heartbeat. Good medicine here is to recognize that interdependence is key to balance.

If you live in a 2 environment it is important to maintain clear, honest communication with those in your space. Clear communication is paramount in order to optimize this energy. Rule of thumb: Say what you mean and mean what you say. Watch out for people-pleasing tendencies and be mindful of expectations.
It isn't unusual for someone in this energy to develop codependent tendencies.

Antidote: Set healthy boundaries. Maintain those boundaries. Ensure your interdependence.

Ideal for:
Couples, newlyweds
Roommates
Business partnerships
Attracting relationships

Unsupportive of:
Home-based businesses
Start-ups
Singles

Complementary Colors:
Orange
Earth tones

Crystals that promote balance and harmony of the mind, body, emotions, and Spirit:
Jade
Smoky Quartz
Blue Lace Agate

Simple tools & tricks for balancing the energy of the 2:
Decorate in a style that represents and combines everyone's tastes.
Create space that invites quality time (cozy living rooms).
Add water! A fountain, pool or small water feature reflects fluidity and balance.

Home Intention for living in the energy of 2:
"Our" home will feel balanced, harmonious, and facilitate reciprocity and interdependence in all experiences.

Work Intention for home-officing in the energy of 2:
"Our" home-office environment will promote equanimity, effective partnerships, and efficiently produce well-rounded outcomes.

#3 ATTRACTION RATHER THAN PROMOTION

The 3 is the most creative of the single digits. Think about it this way: 1 is the individual. 2 is the partnership. 3 is what is born from the partnership. It's the birthing of a new idea, energy, or experience.

The 3-home has pizazz and shine. It contains that "something" you can't put your finger on but that you know you want to be around. The 3 energy cultivates the charismatic vibe of attraction rather than promotion. This energy can also encourage the development of intuition and psychic gifts. #Three's Company

Love to entertain? If your address numerology adds up to 3, your home is a great party house. This is a great space for charming influencers to host guests with hospitality. The 3-home is often the hot-spot in the 'hood where everyone gathers. Even if you're not planning on entertaining, the 3-home certainly brings some sass, optimism, childlike wonder, creativity, and playfulness to the forefront.

Watch out: You can feel so "on" all of the time that it can be draining. Be careful about overdoing things and/or pretending to smile when you're actually feeling down in a 3-space. Lack of self-awareness is typical to feel in a 3-home when it comes to boundaries and limits. Be aware of people-pleasing behaviors in this space.

The 3-home does not offer the same focus, drive and efficiency of the 1. The energy here truly supports the voice of the artist who is driven by inspiration and passion rather than purpose and focus. The vibe can get edgy and complacent or indifferent when there's not enough creativity involved. Any imbalance in creativity

NUMEROLOGY FOR YOUR HOME

can cause the vibe to swing from high to low, which can feel moody. To thine own self be true.

It isn't unusual for someone in this energy to forget healthy self-care practices.

Antidote: Relax. Rejuvenate. Ground. Sleep hygiene is a must.

Ideal for:
Artists
Writers
Media people
Public relations people
Creating an abundant social life and inspiring creativity

Challenging for:
Introverts
Scientists
Health care practitioners
Clinical home-office environments

Complementary Colors:
Yellow
Bright, iridescent color schemes

Crystals that promote energy, vitality, and inspired creativity:
Peridot
Peacock Ore
Pyrite

Simple tools & tricks for balancing the energy of the 3:
Dedicate time to self-care routines.
Recharge yourself with restful sleep.
Play outside in nature as often as possible.

Home Intention for living in the energy of 3:
My home will be filled with fun, joy, community, and wonder-filled experiences, while organically creating space for rest and rejuvenation.

Work Intention for home-officing in the energy of 3:
My home-office environment will inspire creativity, uniqueness, and cutting-edge products, while maintaining a stable foundation.

#4 ORGANIZATION STATION

Places, please! The frequency of the 4-home is all about the putting everything in just the right space. The 4-home promotes neatness and tidiness: there's a place for everything and everything should be in its place. The energy of the 4 has a grid-like quality in that it seeks stability, consistency, and routine as a means of finding satisfaction, success, or even peace. #GetErDone

If you're wanting an organized dwelling or professional home-office space, the number 4 is ideal for you! This energy is process driven and methodical. The frequency of the number 4 will naturally generate a sense of stability and groundedness. If you want to plant some roots and build a solid foundation for your life, a 4-environment will do just that. It offers the perfect frequency for cleaning up clutter (literally, mentally, emotionally, and potentially spiritually).

If your address numerology adds up to 4, this is a home of prioritization, order, and structure. Things are built here, and discipline is refined. The 4-home is ideal if you are working to get your finances on track or live within a reasonable budget. It also supports growing a home-based business by energetically guiding you to implement security and stability throughout all processes. Let's get real: it's a pretty traditional and conventional energy. Nothing wrong with that! We all experience life-stages where it is imperative that we re-vamp and reorganize aspects of our lives in order to build a solid, functional base, and a good platform for success.

Watch out: Control freak tendencies are possible. Yes, the 4-home can promote rigid or staunch views and approaches. Here, boundaries tend to be drawn with a sharpie marker rather than a pencil like the more fluid 3-home. Once a line is drawn in a 4-home, residents can be too proud or controlling to erase the line. The 4 vibe can be like a game of 4 square. Remember that as a kid? If the ball hits the line, it doesn't count. This is the type of energy you'll experience with a 4 home.

Be mindful of obsessive and compulsive behaviors in a 4-home. This isn't the party house—rather, it's a particularly structured environment. That said, it's important to not to be too serious and to invite some fun and playfulness in a 4 space. Be sure to invoke rhythm and balance in your home versus rigidity.

It isn't unusual for someone in this energy to become overly rigid, inflexible, and controlling.

Antidote: Open-mindedness and willingness are key. Find time for play. Chill out.

Ideal for:
Organizing a new home-business model or plan
Developing discipline and routine
CPAs
Lawyers

Challenging for:
Artists
Creativity
Casual, let-it-all-hang-out types
Dreamers
Intuitive and healing work

Complementary Colors:
Green
The basics: black, white and navy

Crystals that promote alignment, productivity, steadiness & stability:
Bloodstone
Tigers Eye
Kyanite

Simple tools & tricks for balancing the energy of the 4:
Make room for a pet (something that is playful and unconditionally loving).
Strategically display items that offer comic relief (funny magnets, coffee table books, sayings).
Let in light! Lots of windows and openness.

Home Intention for living in the energy of 4:

My home offers stability, consistency, and functionality, as well alignment of aspirations with inspiration.

Work Intention for home-officing in the energy of 4:

My home-office environment promotes solid, effective, and lasting foundations, while interconnecting the people with the processes.

#5 LIGHTNING STRIKES TWICE

The 5 is here! The 5 is there! The 5 is going everywhere!
If your address numerology adds up to 5, your home
is all about the adventure. It's a great space for movers
and shakers, and people on the go. The 5-home usually
generates unexpected opportunities. It offers thrill-seeking
energy like an adrenaline-junkie (mentally, emotionally
and physically). The 5 is totally alive! #ReadySetGo

Not looking to nest? 5 is the vibe you want. This is totally
a crash pad or space that you don't plan to get cozy in
for the long-term. The 5-home is all about freedom and
liberation. This is a great environment for entertainment

and excitement. This energy is similar to the extroversion of the 3, however the 3 has the lasting, uplifting effect from a cup of coffee while the 5 is like a jolt from an espresso shot, or two! The 5 environment will have an independent and fearless flare that's always on the go and ready for the next big thing.

Watch out: The residents here can be known to thrive on the next high or insight. If things are calm, stable or consistent, you may feel restless, irritable and discontent in a 5. Thus, drama is sometimes created in order to generate some "excitement." The 5-home residents can find themselves falling into overindulgent and selfish behaviors, always thriving on the next high or even the next low. Be mindful that this energy tends to promote mostly action and little stillness and peace.

5-homes don't have a lot of grey areas. They typically aren't places to find middle ground. 5 is not the ideal environment for cultivating stability or consistency. Rather, it promotes free thinking, and living outside the proverbial box.

5 energy is about taking risks, seizing the moment, and stepping through the doors of opportunity. This is the

environment for change and the place where lightning can strike twice. Adventure appears at every turn. It's an encouraging energy for anyone who feels stagnation and needs to generate some momentum for change.

A key to optimizing this energy is treating the environment as temporary, or short-term. It's an energy that you can tap into to evoke change. This environment is anything but dull. It promotes flexibility, freedom and dynamic force.

It isn't unusual for someone in the 5 energy to lose focus or lack commitment and follow-through.

Antidote: Accountability. Alignment. Find reciprocity in all projects and endeavors.

Ideal for:
Airbnbs
Travelers
People on the go
Someone newly single or coming out of a relationship
Salespeople
Festival headquarters or amusement parks
Camping

Challenging for:

People prone to addictions
A family or newlyweds
Home-officing (typically)
Yoga and meditation

Complementary Colors:

Blue
Silver
White
Colors that sparkle

Crystals that promote balance, flow, stability, and adaptability:

Carnelian
Petrified Wood
Moonstone

Simple tools & tricks for balancing the energy of 5:

Meditate. Meditate. Meditate.
Volunteer and find ways to be of service to others.
Identify what or who promotes stability and incorporate them often.

Home Intention for living in the energy of 5:
My home promotes adaptability, adventure, and freedom, while allowing me to experience stability, accountability, and peace.

Work Intention for home-officing in the energy of the 5:
This home-office environment will foster excitement, optimism, and adventure, constantly shifting and changing to meet the needs of the client.

#6 THE NESTER

Comfort. Companionship. Nurturing. That is the energy of the 6. The 6 is truly the gentlest of the single digits, enveloping tolerance, compassion and unconditional love in its highest vibe. If you look at the 6 with your imaginative eye, it could be representative of a pregnant woman. So think of it figuratively as the mother figure. #HomeIsWhereTheHeartIs

If your address numerology adds up to 6, you are living in the ultimate nesting space. This is the energy of home and family. Your house naturally evokes a genuinely warm, loving and caring essence. 6 is the quintessential homey feel that is inviting and filled with love. Like the 3, this environment inspires creativity, but it offers authentic connection through love and unity. Inside the 6-house you naturally feel at home. It's an easy space to enjoy a cup of coffee, sit around the dinner table and visit, or cozy up next to the fireplace with a good book.

Need advice? This is likely an environment where you can get it. This space is quite the charmer. If you are in need of focusing on self-care and health, this is an organic environment in which to do so. Your innate compassion will rise to the surface in a 6-home.

Watch out: Mom-types can be overprotective, self-sacrificing, nit-picky, gossipy, and overly sensitive. Those in a 6-home can give and give of itself to the point of martyrdom and forget the most important lesson: Take care of yourself, or you won't be able to take care of anyone else. Be aware of codependent tendencies and controlling, manipulative, attention-seeking behaviors that can quietly emerge in a 6-home. Helicopter parenting and micromanaging roommates are potential problems to work through with this energy.

It is not unusual for people in 6 environments to develop a need to fix, save, or rescue those around them.

Antidote: Oxygen mask. Self-Care. Always put your oxygen mask on first and then you can assist someone else.

Ideal for:
Families
Newlyweds
Healers
Counselors
Yogis

Challenging for:
College students or young adults
People needing structure and process
People who travel for business
People with addictive behaviors

Complementary Colors:
Pink
Light and neutral colors

Crystals that promote love, tolerance, compassion, and security:
Rose Quartz
Amethyst or Chevron Amethyst
Tourmaline

Simple tools & tricks for balancing the energy of 6:
Set up personal space for "me time."
Use a planner to stay on task and organize time.
Make time for leisurely travel and adventures.

Home Intention for living in the energy of 6:
I feel at home, safe, secure, and authentic in this environment and in my own skin.

Work Intention for home-officing in the energy of 6:
This work environment feels comfortable, nurturing, and promotes health, well-being, and community.

#7 THE PASSIONATE PATH OF PURSUIT

The energy of a 7-home is passionate, highly personal, and has a more serious tone that can ignite spiritual development. This is great energy for someone developing their spiritual and metaphysical practices. If you are focusing on learning about consciousness, seeking expansion and developing heightened awareness of what exists beyond our physical reality, the 7-home will certainly aid your journey. This energy is where mystics, professors or anyone in pursuit of higher aspirations around knowledge will thrive. #BloomWhereYourePlanted

If your address numerology adds up to 7, your residents may take on the role of the seeker, always in search of something higher, deeper, and often on the spiritual plane. The 7-home brings out the philosopher, the knight on the quest for the holy grail, and the researcher in pursuit of wisdom, knowledge, and truth.

The 7-home feels analytical and yet usually attracts the more mysterious side of life. This energy takes nothing at face value and is on the search for truth and enlightenment. While this energy promotes self-reflection, it may also breed isolation and introversion. The thought-provoking, insightful nature of the 7-home can also be quite secretive.

Watch out: The 7-home can have you so focused on the pursuit of knowledge that you forget the outside world exists. Residents can be stuck in their head, overly critical, and never satisfied. If you tend to hang on to things and generate clutter in your home or home-office space, this vibration will magnify that if you're not careful (you'd be better off in a 4-home that would encourage organization).

This is not the place you will go for gossip, small talk or idle chatter. The 7-home residents can feel like they are struggling on an endless pursuit without fulfillment or completion. Be careful not to get lost in your mind in a 7-home. Be sure to incorporate fun and the unexpected into this environment.

It is not unusual for the 7 energy to hoard things and harbor ideas, which can breed dishonesty and mistrust.

Antidote: Collaboration. Connection. Reach out and find groups of people with similar interests to share ideas and fellowship.

Ideal for:
Writers
Professors
Researchers
Spiritual Teachers
Seekers
Home-Schooling

Challenging for:
People prone to addictions or obsessive behaviors
Families

Complementary Colors:
Indigo
Gray
Matte color palette

Crystals that promote intelligence, honest communication, calmness, and clarity:
Fluorite
Lapis Lazuli
Hematite

Simple tools & tricks for balancing the energy of the 7:
Create a vision board, keeping your dreams alive.
Declutter wherever and whenever possible. Schedule it if you must.
Allow natural light and open windows to open up this space.

Home Intention for living in the energy of the 7:
In this home, I will experience purpose-driven development, an expanded consciousness, and a heightened awareness of my reality, while finding balance in interactions with like-minded thinkers.

Work Intention for home-officing in the energy of the 7:
This working environment will promote a rich experience in the pursuit of higher knowledge and innovation, while tapping into the ever-expanding stream of consciousness and the collective.

#8 RISK & REWARD

If you turn the 8 on its side, what do you get? The infinity symbol. The number 8 is the number of balance and power: it is a closed circuit, never beginning or ending. Residents of an 8-home are learning to find value in fluidity, and how to recognize the relationship between the material and immaterial world. #GoForTheGold

If you are self-employed or an entrepreneur, 8 is the place for you! The 8-home exudes abundance and power, so any financial endeavor will likely have the momentum it needs in order to materialize with prosperity. Wait. Does this sound too good to be true? With the 8 there can be great reward; however, on the flip side, there can also be great loss. This environment is a no pain, no gain kind of deal. With big risk, there is big reward. You cannot sit on the sidelines in the 8 energy. It's also the same for physical fitness; 8 is an ideal vibration for athletes who are diligent in training and competing for big wins.

The 1-home is the ideal place for initiating or starting a new life or home business endeavor. However, the energy of the 8-home is what you want to utilize once you begin building momentum and have a solid foundation or effective practices in place (the 4 is the ideal vibe for establishing these important traits). I don't recommend the 8 at the beginning of a new home building endeavor. It's a more mature vibration that takes finesse, because you can easily get pulled down by any small amount of negative momentum. Again, this is the risk and reward ratio vibe. It is an energy that is continually moving and must be assessed and reassessed.

If your address numerology adds up to 8, your home can feel like a roller coaster of thoughts, experiences and emotions. Rather than approaching this energy like a thrill-seeker, think of it like riding a wave. Learn to go with the flow and feel alive. Be like a leaf on a fast moving stream, ready to move at all times. Be willing to gain renewed perspective from all of the experiences (high and low) and find gratitude in the present. Be encouraged to trust in the nature of change.

Watch Out: Residents of the 8-home can get caught up in the high highs and the low lows. Trust and empowerment may not be innate tools of the 8 energy, but they are the very key to magnificent, off the charts manifestation.

The number 8 is always moving and expanding. More space. More things. More people. More... you get the picture. Because of this, be aware of tendencies toward dissatisfaction and ingratitude.

It is not unusual for the energy of the 8 to thrive on the high-highs and low-lows.

Antidote: Middle Ground. Peace and Serenity. Discover the empowerment (not power and ego) of the present moment.

Ideal for:

Entrepreneurs

Athletes

Brokers & Agents

Risk takers

Challenging for:

Families

Scientists

Accountants

Healing Professionals

Complementary Colors:

Dark Blues

Magenta

Greens

Crystals that promote empowerment, stamina, fluidity, and flexibility:

Citrine

Opal

Topaz

Simple tools & tricks for balancing the energy of an 8:
Find ways to be of service when no one is looking.
Give credit to others, always and often.
Use incense, candles, essential oils to soften the
environment, promoting peace and stillness.

Home Intention for living in the energy of the 8:
This home will generate an abundant experience,
and promote a consciousness of innate wealth, while
organically fostering security and peace within.

Work Intention for home-officing in the energy of the 8:
This environment will feel exciting and invigorating,
continually renewing vitality and energy, and will
promote expanded consciousness and abundant
perspective through change.

#9 THE GREAT CONNECTION

If your address numerology adds up to 9, your residents are learning integrity, innate wisdom, leadership and above all, surrender. The 9-home embodies greatness and purpose. It is an all-inclusive vibe that promotes our connectedness, exudes clarity, and enhances intuition.

The 9 comes with quite a hefty experience: It is the last of the single digit numbers and thus incorporates or embodies all of the lessons and vibrations of the numbers that come before it. #FullCircle

In a 9-home residents feel called to rise to the occasion of the day. Living in this energy can be intense, exhausting and feel overly burdensome. Think of it as an environment that promotes high standards: greatness is imminent coupled with an underlying sense of urgency.

The 9-home promotes the energy of wise counsel. If you are in the business of giving advice, well, this environment is totally your jam. Consider too, that this may not be the type of energy you want for your home because you could be tempted to take work home with you.

The 9-home has built-in charisma, influence, and stature which attracts nearly all walks of life. This is a relatable and familiar energy. Residents in the 9-home can identify with any average Joe on the street or the leading CEO in any industry. The 9-home, however, is not the ideal space for the jokester or thrill-seeker, nor is it the party house.

Watch out: Doesn't the above sound like a lot of burden and responsibility? If you lack self-awareness it sure can be. It's important to learn how to to release unrealistic expectations of yourself and others in this space. If you don't, you can find yourself becoming overly critical and way to intense to be around. Be aware that you can also feel an imaginary yet very real sense of urgency in a 9-home, as though you're running out of time.

It is not unusual to feel an extraordinary sense of urgency as if the weight of the world is on your shoulders in a 9-home.

Antidote: Let go. Surrender. Find freedom in releasing outdated belief systems. Laugh, and laugh as often as possible.

Ideal for:
Community-oriented people
Eco-villages
Support-services professionals
Counselors
Film-makers
Leaders
Humanitarians & philanthropists

Challenging for:
Environments with children & teenagers
Over-achievers
Perfectionists
People prone to depression
People with naturally high anxiety

Complementary Colors:
Gold
Amber
Bronze
Silver
The metals

Crystals that promote steady energy, the release of self-imposed limitations, and the insight to access innate wisdom:
Unakite Jasper
Larimar
Aragonite

Simple tools & tricks for balancing the energy of the 9:
Journal, journal, journal, and journal some more.
Create a space that enhances happiness and joy.
Connect with others as often as possible.
Play fun, upbeat dance music, often.

Home Intention for living in the energy of 9:
This home will embody unconditional love, joy, and unity, while sustaining integrity, trust, and the ability to let go of what no longer serves the highest good.

Work Intention for home-officing in the energy of 9:
This environment will exude integrity, strength, and leadership, while naturally shedding outdated systems and processes in order to promote the highest efficacy in all applications.

"To live a pure unselfish life, one must count nothing as one's own in the midst of abundance."

-Buddha

THE MASTER NUMBERS

What about addresses that equal a master number?
Double the risk—double the reward.

Master numbers and repeating numbers are all around
us: in our birthdays, addresses, on the clock, odometer,
speed limit, and on and on. They are codes that we can
utilize and harness to tap into our highest potential.
We access these number codes optimally if we also
incorporate the mastery or wisdom of the base number.

The master numbers are 11, 22, and 33. With master
numbers you have added strengths and opportunities for
"mastery," coupled with added challenges and sensitivity

or vulnerabilities. There is more potential inherent in the master numbers than in the single digits.

The base number is what you get when you reduce each master number down to one digit. I'll show you more about each base number in the examples below. People tend to overlook this important factor: Understanding the base vibration is part of mastering the energy of master numbers. The rule of thumb here is to first and always, reduce the repeating digits down to its base number (or single digit). You want to ensure that the base number is compatible with your goals and that you are understanding and incorporating the characteristics and lessons from the base number first. Then, you can tap into the enhanced mastery that the energy of the master number offers.

In address numerology, it is best to test the base number first and feel comfortable and confident in its energy before changing your address code to a master number. Do you have to do this? No. However, I've found that when people jump straight into the vibration of a master number with no context or experience it can be exhausting, breed frustration, intensity and even feelings or experiences of failure. If you add your address up and it equals a master number, that's totally cool, and likely an omen inviting you into some sort of mastery.

Clarification: Often people think 44, 55, 66 and so on are master numbers. Yes, these numbers do carry more power than a single digit. However, in general numerology, they are not considered master numbers. Numbers that repeat more than twice (222, 333, 444, and so on), also have a higher vibration, impact, and intensity. Yet, they are not master numbers.

11 = MASTER OF ILLUMINATION

BASE # 2

The 11 is called the psychic's number. It's the master of illumination. The double 1 is the representation of where the human world and the spirit world meet. Because it's base is a 2, this energy is the highest form of collaboration and connection.

This is the "aha" of all numbers. 11 is the most intuitively oriented of the Abundance Codes, thus an 11 space offers an invitation to master synchronicity and connection in everything. Rapid manifestation is a blessing and a curse in this environment. If you are thinking and feeling uplifted, then that's what your environment will reflect.

Watch out: If you are in a state of anxiety or restlessness, you will experience those attributes directly in your environment. 11 energy can be highly uncomfortable and even detrimental for those who are not on a spiritual path. The key is finding focus, clarity, and balance. Seek alignment in an 11 environment. Get it? We are tapping into the 2 with the balance and alignment piece while harnessing the compounding energy and spiritual mastery of the 11.

Complementary Colors:
Silver
Sparkles & Glitter
Violet

Crystals that promote psychic abilities, integration of insight, and balance of energies:
Lepidolite
Herkimer Diamond
Iolite

Simple tools & tricks for grounding the energy of the 11:
Review and re-review your intentions/goals/desires, checking them against your experience.
Ground. Get outside and connect with the earth regularly.
Clear the energy in the house often with sage or palo santo.

Home Intention for living in the energy of 11:
This home will align me with my human self and my higher self, continuously refocusing my mind, body, emotions, and spirit with a higher calling.

Work Intention for home-officing in the energy of 11:
This environment will promote cosmic connections and expanded consciousness. I can easily access higher levels of awareness in every project, task, and responsibility.

22 = MASTER BUILDER

BASE # 4

The 22 is the master builder. This environment is all about turning hopes and dreams into a tangible reality. Because this energy is built on the foundation of stability in the 4, the energy in a 22-home helps bring big concepts to life that are built to last.

Watch out: The energy of the 22 builds on the 11, turning intuition into clear, focused reality. Be mindful of unnecessary pressure, hyper-focus, and overly critical thinking in a 22 environment. If everyone in the space is not aligned with a higher calling and sense of purpose, this energy can breed competition, control, and limited perspectives. The highest way to utilize the energy of a 22 environment is to be of practical service.

22 is a powerful vibration and not usually supportive of the novice. When you choose the 22 for your home environment, you want to have trust, faith, and belief in yourself or your cause. When in doubt, play with the 4 first!

Complementary Colors:
Gold
Red
Black
Anything that "looks" solid or grounding (not necessarily patterns or floral prints)

Crystals that promote positive flow, release of obsessive thought-patterns, and stable manifestation:
Dalmatian Stone
Peridot
Coral

Simple tools & tricks for grounding the energy of the 22:
Review and re-review your processes and organization, checking them against your experience.
Ground. Get outside and connect with the Earth regularly.

Find stability and consistency in the day-to-day (intend it, look for it, utilize it).

Clear the energy in the house often with sage or palo santo.

Home Intention for living in the energy of the 22:
This home will transform my dreams into a solid, stable, and enduring reality while constructing an abundant environment.

Work Intention for home-officing in the energy of the 22:
This environment will build something that will last—with a solid, strategic vision—and organically generate effective tools and resources to follow through with fulfillment and abundance.

33 = MASTER HEALER OR TEACHER
BASE # 6

33 is the master healer. In a 33 environment, you are invited to inspire others by sharing your innate wisdom. Because the base energy of the 6 is about self-love, a 33 space supports tapping into your own creativity first in order to radiate that essence around you. This is the energy where you can truly learn to embody the essence of what you want to co-create in your reality and life.

The 33-home evokes an innate essence of influence. The 33 frequency is highly experiential and will show you rather than tell you. What does that mean? You experience things first rather than planning them and intellectually analyzing or orchestrating them. Literally, it's like having a blindfold on and learning to feel, trust and rely on the senses you may not typically use in maneuvering most situations. Residents of a 33-home are required to summon their inner Luke Skywalker.

Watch out: This number may border on perfectionism and be quite challenging. You may not catch a breath (or a break) in this space. Why? It's an environment of a lot of feeling and intuition, where you will be encouraged to choose unconditional love versus finding the proverbial strings to attach to your love. A key to maximizing this energy is being aware of unreasonable expectations of yourself and others. Also, be mindful of over analyzing situations and having a "need to know." Trust. Believe. You can thrive in this environment and even stimulate evolutionary changes in the world around you and beyond.

Complementary Colors:
Blues
Greens
Turquoise
Iridescent Color Pallet

Crystals that promote trust, faith, and patience in addition to consistency with flexibility:
Azurite
Chrysocolla
Malachite

Simple tools & tricks for grounding the energy of the 33:
Review and re-review and release your expectations of yourself and others, checking them against your experience.
Ground. Be present. Get outside and connect with the Earth regularly.
Salt and crystal baths for cleansing your energy and emotional body.
Clear the energy in the house often with sage or palo santo.

Home Intention for living in the energy of 33:
In this home, I allow and trust the flow of my experiences to guide me and those sharing this space in the experience of unconditional love, gratitude, and peace, in line with the greatest good.

Work Intention for home-officing in the energy of 33:
This environment will create a healthy, healing, and unconditional space for the upliftment of those co-existing in it, producing outcomes aligned with the highest good.

What if I have an address that contains repeating Master Numbers?

For example: 222 Peace Street.

Yes, there is an added element of intensity and personification through the triple 2, but this is not a master number, as discussed above. However, it does have 22 (the master builder) in it and the triple personification of the 2. What does that mean?

First: Examine the energy of the 2. It's about collaboration and relationship.

Second: Sum it up: $2 + 2 + 2 = 6$.

Here we have the energy of the 6, which represents the base or fundamental energy of nurturing, self-care and unconditional love.

Look at how the 2 and the 6 relate. What do you get from that? There is a theme of compassion, tolerance and unconditional love that will be relatable (relationship = 2) in this environment.

Don't get too caught up in repeating digits in the actual address. Rather, examine how the repeating master number affects your environment and what lesson it may be calling forth.

"Abundance is not something we acquire. It is something we tune into."

-Wayne Dyer

CHANGING THE ENERGY OF YOUR ADDRESS WITHOUT MOVING

Changing the vibration of your home is super simple. Seriously, it just takes a few steps, and does not require you to contact the post office. All it takes is a post-it note!

First:
Determine what energy you're wanting to bring into your home life. This is no small thing—it requires discernment of your goals and desires. Carefully review the traits of the numbers in the previous chapters to help you decide what energetic frequency and which number you'd like to call in to your space. Take into consideration what you already have going for you, and what you would like to

create in terms of making your life easier, more vibrant, or more focused, etc. Tune in to your intuition. Feel your feelings. Take a look at your dreams.

Let's say that you decide you are going to take a major turn in your life. For example, you are leaving a corporate job and starting your own business where you will be working from home. You may want to ensure that your new home-officing environment promotes a focused, business-oriented atmosphere to support your new endeavor. The simplest suggestion is changing your address to an 8. As a reminder the 8-home is about big risks, big rewards, and riding the waves of change with fluidity. You might also consider changing your address numerology to a 4 or 1, depending on your goals and the nature of your endeavor. But for simplicity, 8 is a power number for home-based businesses and entrepreneurs.

Second:
Once you've determined what number you want to use, take the sum of your current address and figure out what number you would need to add to it so that the sum would reduce down to the number you want. Let's continue with the example of the 8.

Say your address is currently 4503 Winding Springs Road. Your current address vibration would be a 3.

Why is it a 3?

4 + 5 + 0 + 3 = 12
1 + 2 = 3

What we want is an 8.

So, what do you add to 3 to equal 8?

The answer is 5.
(5 + 3 = 8)

Third:

Now that you know you want to add a 5 to your address to change the vibration of your home to an 8, do you go outside and add a 5 to the address on your mailbox? Merciful heavens, no you do not! The post office would have a fit. And it wouldn't do your address numerology any good either! No, leave the mailbox alone. There's another way—and it's so simple it's almost hysterical—however, it totally works.

All you do is get a post-it note and write the number 5 on it.

[Do not simply write the number you're wanting—which in this case is 8. <u>This will not work,</u> and you will affect the numerology in a completely different way than you are intending to change.]

Stick the post-it note with the 5 written on it to the inside of the doorframe of your front door.

Yes, that's all you have to do! Trust me, it works. Give it a week or two (sometimes it can be sooner) and you will begin to notice shifts in the energy. Put your intentions to work and trust the process. Change happens in the energy field of your home. Every time. You can feel it. It's magical—but a quantum physicist will tell you that it's just good science theory at work.

Let's do a more complex example:

Say your address is currently: 2375 Unit 4E Steeple Chase Lane.

Your current address numerology is an 8 and you want to change it to a 6.

Why is it currently an 8?

$2 + 3 + 7 + 5 + 4 + 5$ (E = 5 in the alphabet chart) $= 26$

$2 + 6 = 8$

What do you add to 8 to reduce down to 6?

The answer is 7. Why?

$8 + 7 = 15$

$1 + 5 = 6$

Got it? Good. You're on your way to greater abundance. Got questions? Read on.

HOW DO I APPLY THIS?

Practical Advice & Tips

I encourage you to play with the energies of your address. It's important to figure out what you are striving to enhance or promote in your living space—your home. Obviously, you want to make good choices. But this is not a dive off the high board into the shallow end of the pool. It's more like putting on water wings and learning how to swim with the possibilities. Play with it slowly. Once you make a change, leave your address numerology alone for several months (at least 6). This is about creating an environment that supports your dreams and desires.

You don't have to do this alone. The universe can and will support you in this if you put in a little thought and intentionality behind it. All you are wanting to do first, is to find the energies that will make your life richer, fulfilling and more abundant. More fun.

1. How do you figure out what you desire?

Questions to Ponder

How do I want to feel in this space?
What is my goal in this environment?
Am I seeking mental clarity and efficient use of time?
Do I want to feel more nourished at home?
Do I need a crash pad to bounce out of for travel?
Am I at a time in my life where I'm needing to spend
more time focusing inward on spiritual things?
What do I want to shift or create more of in this space?
What relationships do I have going on in this space?
Are others' goals and desires in line with mine in my
home?

2. Find the number that best matches that description.

Example: Looking for Love, Fun, or Adventure

Question to ask yourself: What do I want to attract into
my life?

If you are a single person living alone and want to
attract a more robust social life—possibly a romantic
relationship or new connections/friendships—the logical
options are 2, 3 or 5.

#2 - If you are currently single and looking for love and partnership, changing the vibe to a 2 will organically promote (in your energetic field and your environment) an openness to relationship and connection. By dwelling and marinating in the 2 energy, you will feel more naturally aware of how you relate to the people in your life and become more attuned to the people who cross your path. This shift changes your personal magnetic energy field towards an openness to partnership and connection. In other words, you're telling the universe that you're ready for a relationship through the language of frequency.

#3 - If your goal is to incorporate more fun, festive, and social energies into your environment, the 3 is ideal. It will change the vibe of your home to encourage you to entertain and invite people into your space (both your literal home and out in life). This is a great environment for attracting more people and more fun into your life.

#5 - If you are looking for more adventure, travel, and opportunity, the 5 is the ticket! Now, with the 5, remember it is an energy that is not keen on stagnation or rest and rejuvenation—it is truly for someone who is ready to "not be at home"—someone who wants to get out and experience life through new adventures.

Example: Healing Vibes

Question to ask: What do I want to focus on to improve my health/lifestyle?

If you want to improve your health and wellbeing, the logical options are 1, 4, 6, or 7.

#1 - If you are wanting to get in shape, eat better, feel better, and commit to a lifestyle overhaul, the 1 is probably the number for you. By utilizing the energy of the 1—which will encourage focus, dedication, drive, and commitment—you will feel supported to set health goals for yourself and take the necessary actions for follow-through. Just watch out for overzealous goals and workaholic behaviors. Be reasonable and take it easy, one day at a time.

#4 - If your goal is cleaning up your current lifestyle and revamping unhealthy behavioral patterns that hold you back from optimal health and wellness, the 4 is a fabulous energy to tap into more structure. It will foster cleaning up attitudes, actions, and the overall environment, while helping you feel supported in establishing a new lifestyle. If you have an addictive personality or tendencies, I would encourage tapping into the 4 rather than the 1 to keep you focused on healthy routines and processes that support overall wellbeing.

#6 - If your goal is healthy self-care and mental health, the 6 may be a good option for you to consider. Because the 6 is the most unconditional of the numbers, it can assist you in shifting any negative perceptions of yourself and clean up unhealthy self-talk or shaming - as long as you set your intentions around these issues. The 6-home will offer compassion and kindness to residents in a soft and subtle way. However, with the nurturing and sentient energy of the 6, it is important not to become overly sensitive. Be aware of your emotions. Set clear boundaries and find balance with your self-care practices. Put the oxygen mask on yourself first, and then you can help others.

#7 - If you want to focus on enriching your spirituality and karmic healing, then the 7 energy is intense but worth the the energetic exploration. The 7-home will encourage you to dive deep into the spiritual and metaphysical and possibly guide you in attracting like-minded seekers into your life. This energy can open up an expansive and rich inner-life, propelling your spiritual journey in this lifetime, and exposing you to new personal truths. Be mindful of overly introverted behaviors. Make sure to get out and test your self-discovery in the real world. As Pierre Teilhard de Chardin observed, "we are not human beings having a spiritual experience—we are spiritual beings having a human experience."

Tip: Remember, you can change your address numerology if it is not feeling like a good match or if your goals change, which they inherently will. Choose a number that is most applicable and practical to accomplishing your current goals and desires. Commit to the number for at least 6 months—this is imperative to effecting the change, integrating it, and optimizing results.

Example: Nesting

My home address adds up to a 5. 5 energy is all about adventure, dynamic shifts and changes. When I first moved into this home, I was a newlywed. My logical choices were to shift our address numerology from a

5-home to a 2-home or 6-home. I chose 6 because both my husband and I are naturally on-the-go people. My job involved traveling a vast majority of the time and my husband is not one to sit still. So, I chose the number 6, the nester, because I wanted to create an environment we looked forward to coming home to and spending quality time together. I also wanted to encourage an environment where we felt nurtured, loved, and safe.

Guess what else? It worked so well I kept the address a 6 vibration for almost 3 years! We were able to spend that time learning how to understand each other, develop compassion as a couple and interdependently, and create space for understanding, support, and unconditional love. This environment also guided me in healthy self-care—knowing when to stay home, take a sea salt bath, relax, and rest. All of these are part of a routine that, today, is paramount to my balance and well-being as an individual and in a partnership.

3. Recognize the downfalls or challenges associated with the new number.

Be sure you understand the "bad behaviors" and challenges associated with the number you choose.

Take those into account. Acknowledging these limiting attitudes is important so that you can identify them when they creep up in your life with mindfulness. This way, you are engaged with the energetic feedback, and poised to modify behaviors and thoughts to regain balance. It's also interesting to track the changes when they occur.

Practice setting intentions around balancing the negative traits of those energies. When you notice a negative vibe, it is a personal growth opportunity, not a set-back. Set new intentions, intentionally!

Personal Example: When I changed my address numerology to a 6, I realized one of the associated limiting behaviors had emerged for me in the form of people-pleasing. Rather than speaking my truth or my preferences, I would put my wants, needs, and desires on the back burner and acquiesce to those of my husband and sometimes others. Next, I would develop resentment. Definitely a bad vibe. How did that happen? It could be something as simple as the following:

My husband: "I'm going to xyz place and run a couple of errands, do you want to come with me?"

Me: "Sure." (I would say "sure," yet I might have been tired after a long day/week of work and travel and really might have wanted to say "no." However, I would say yes because I felt it would let him down or somehow dissatisfy him—which was totally untrue).

This behavior went on for a full year. Yes, that long! Once I recognized the pattern, I became intentional about countering it: "I trust my voice and maintain interdependence in all relationships and situations." Voila! I was able to start saying what I meant and meaning what I said in my relationship with my husband and beyond while learning what negative traits I needed to conquer within the 6-home. Win/win. Progress, not perfection. Breakthrough, not breakdown.

4. Set intentions to balance the energy of the number and incorporate its optimal energies into the environment.

On the opposite page are examples for balancing intentions for each of the numbers.

#1 I am open-minded, patient, and tolerant with myself and those around me.

#2 I set and maintain healthy boundaries in all aspects of my life and relationships.

#3 Rest, relaxation, and healthy self-care come naturally to me.

#4 I am open-minded and willing to relinquish control, effortlessly allowing ease and flow into my life.

#5 I am accountable and consistent and easily create balance in all areas of my life.

#6 I trust my voice and maintain interdependence in all relationships and situations.

#7 Collaboration, connection, and the sharing of ideas happens organically and feels enlightening.

#8 I experience peace and serenity in the present, while creating stability and consistency.

#9 Joy, happiness, and fun are priorities in my life and allow me to feel free.

5. Commit to the new number you choose for at least 6 months.

I know, this wasn't what you wanted to hear. Everyone loves a quick fix and immediate gratification—me included. Be patient. Allow the energies to take effect. Commit to at least 6 to 8 months. This is how you will experience the most effective and lasting results.
I promise!

"Abundance is a process of letting go; that which is empty can receive."

-Bryant H. McGill

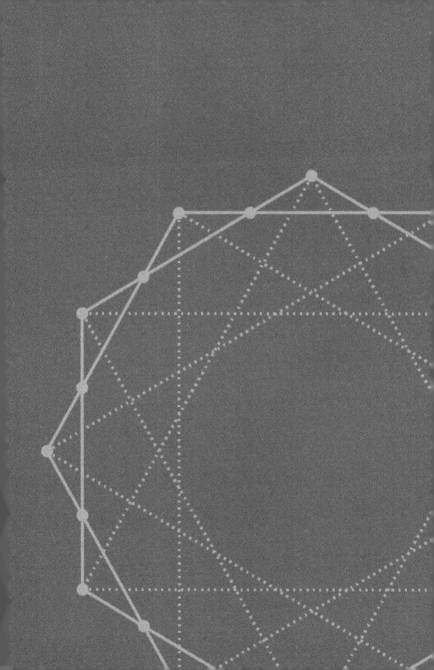

HOUSE CLEARING

Once you've changed your address numerology, the space will start to take on a new frequency. It can be helpful to move the old energy out and welcome the new energy in with a house clearing. Below is my colleague and dear friend Tiffany Harelik's recipe for clearing your house, as she describes in the companion book *Astrology for your Home: Using Planetary Patterns to Shift Your Life*.

Pro-tip: consider ushering the new energy in with your post-it note on a New Moon. The New Moon is an astrological secret weapon to plant seeds for what you want to grow and to receive cosmic help in nourishing those seeds to take root. Behind-the-scenes forces and frequencies align to help you start something new during the first 8 hours of a New Moon. Using astrology in tandem with address numerology is a super power!

Here's what you do:

1. Write the intention that goes with the number you want to bring in on the back of your post-it note. Remember, your post-it note is not 'the number' you want, rather it's the number you need to add to your current address to create 'the number' you want. You may add any of your own intentions at this time (no more than 10 total). For added potency, write these intentions during the first 8 hours of a New Moon.

2. Place crystals that go with the energy of your new address numerology on top of the post-it note and let it sit while you clean your house.

3. Clean your house to the best of your ability. At the very least make sure you have swept all corners and dusted all surfaces. I recommend using organic cleaning solutions, and natural solutions such as vinegar and basil when possible. Magical Housekeeping: Simple Charms and Practical Tips for Creating a Harmonious Home by Tess Whitehurst is one of my favorite books and offers several

strategies to incorporate herbs and crystals into your mopping and cleaning to add more mojo to your space.

4. Perk up your house. Fluff pillows, put dishes away, add a cute new decoration, light some white candles (or coordinate your candle color with the suggested colors that go with your new address number). Yet another way to amplify the astro-numerology! Creating Sacred Space With Feng Shui: Learn the Art of Space Clearing and Bring New Energy into Your Life by Karen Kingston is a wonderful addition to your library as you're learning how to create your ideal home space.

5. Light some sage and gently blow the smoke from your sage wand throughout the house, making sure not to miss closets, space under the bed, and corners. Do this safely and carefully. Be mindful that you may set off the fire or smoke alarm. Lord knows I have scared the neighbors with an overzealous smudge and smoke alarm I couldn't shut off.

6. f you have any bells, singing bowls, or rattles, use them to make a joyful noise in the corners of your home. You can also clap your hands if you don't have any of the other tools available. This ancient shamanic practice

of sound clearing has been used for centuries to clear bad energy, create sacred space, and request spiritual protection.

8. Sprinkle sea salt around the exterior perimeter of your home. This practice wards off negative energy and seals and protects your home in a sacred healing chamber.

9. Turn on your favorite music that goes with the tone you're intending to create with your new address numerology.

10. Speak your intentions aloud, and post the number/ intention up on your front door.

After you clear your house, the stagnant, old energy will be cleansed and transformed. By clearing your house, you've set the stage for some big astro-numerology magic to happen. You may wish to journal your experience for several months, paying close attention to themes around the intentions you set.

Caution: Be aware that house clearing is a powerful practice. You are stirring the pot on the etheric realms and not all unwanted spiritual energy will simply leave.

If you have an unusual circumstance where you feel your house is haunted, it may be beneficial to reach out to a professional who can help you clear your house once and for all.

"Your most precious, valued possessions and your greatest powers are invisible and intangible. No one can take them. You, and you alone, can give them. You will receive abundance for your giving."

-W. Clement Stone

THE ABUNDANCE CODE OF YOUR CAR, CAMPER, OR RV

Does my car have an Abundance Code? Yes, it totally does! There is a reason you feel different vibes driving different cars—your vehicle has its own frequency and its own energetic state. And while you may think the purpose of your car is to safely get you from point A to point B, consider, too, how you can effectively use your time in your car to crack your Abundance Code and add extra vitality to your day.

For example, if you're driving a car that contains a more aggravated energy, this could result in extra (and unnecessary) frustration during peak traffic times. I have a friend who drives a 5 car and her road rage is considerably more elevated than average. It's possible to create the energy you want to feel in your car, camper, or RV with the same basic approach you learned in the address numerology section.

There are several numbers associated with your car: your driver license, your vehicle identification number, your mileage, and even the weight of your tires. But your license plate is what you will use to determine the numerology of your car, camper, or RV and is the most effective way to shift the vibe in alignment of your desires, goals, and dreams.

Once you know the numerology of your vehicle, you gain an understanding of the energetic vibration by learning more about the traits of its base number.

1	2	3	4	5	6	7	8	9
A	B	C	D	E	F	G	H	I
J	K	L	M	N	O	P	Q	R
S	T	U	V	W	X	Y	Z	

For example:

License Plate: BC5 – X489

For letters, refer again to the Pythagorean Alphabet Numerology Chart:

B = 2
C = 3
X = 6

2 + 3 + 5 + 6 + 4 + 8 + 9 = 37

3 + 7 = 10

1 + 0 = 1

The energy of the car is a 1. This car is all about the focus and the "drive." You'll get where you're going in this car.

How do I change the energy of my car?

Like the address, you can add a number to the current code (in this case it's a 1), in order to change the vibration.

1. Decide what type of energy you want in your car, and figure out the correlating number of the energy that you desire.

2. Figure out what number you need to add to the current number (your license plate code) in order to equal the number that you want.

3. Write the number you "need" (in order to make the number you "want") on a post-it note, just like you did with your home address. [Do not simply write the number you're wanting. This will not work, and you will affect the numerology in a completely different way than you are intending.]

4. Tape the post-it note with the number on it inside the driver's side door panel near the vehicle identification number.

With the example above, let's say you have a long commute to and from work—a couple of hours a day—and want to spend that time productively on your personal development. You might consider changing the energy of the car to a 7, which will promote self-reflection, introspection, and accessing higher wisdom.

In order to turn the 1 energy of your car into a 7, you will need to add a 6.

Why add 6?

1 + 6 = 7

Write the number 6 down on your post-it note and tape it inside the driver's side door panel above or near the vehicle identification sticker.

Extra advice for campers and RVs: Use the license plate as the main 'address' vibe. However, if you're camped in a permanent slot at a trailer park, that address must be factored in as well. Combining addresses with license plates is an advanced topic. Reach out to a professional numerologist for help with your goals if you're feeling overwhelmed with the possibilities.

Pro-tip: You can clear the energy of your car, camper, or RV just like you can clear the energy of your house.

1. Take your vehicle through a car wash, or do a thorough cleaning inside and out at home.

2. Fluff up the energy of your car by taking care of it—get an oil change if needed, air up the tires, install new wiper blades, make sure your washer fluid is full, get a full tank of gas.

3. Put a stick of palo santo or your favorite herb or wood near the air conditioning so you get a fresh, earthy scent throughout your car each time you turn on the air conditioning or heat.

4. Optimize the timing of putting your post-it note up within the first 8 hours of the New Moon.

"The key to abundance
is meeting limited
circumstances with
unlimited thoughts."

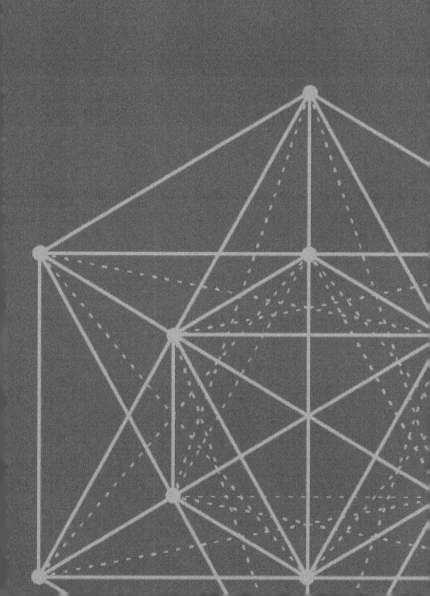

FFAQS: FUN, FREQUENTLY ASKED QUESTIONS:

Are you starting to see that any set of number codes attached to your life has certain energies you may or may not be harnessing? This is the point at which you not only crack your own Abundance Code, you break it wide open. These observations and efforts—with small shifts— are how you make course corrections in attracting your abundance mentality. This is your opportunity to tap into and create an entirely new life.

Is there a way I can mess this up?

Not really . . . but if things feel awry, there's a fix for that!

Do not simply write the number you're wanting. This will not work, and you will affect the numerology in a completely different way than what you are intending. Make sure you follow the instructions. Also, this is about "intention," an important tool for aiding a shift in consciousness to align with your highest aims. Optimize this tool with focus, clarity, and true intention. Also, don't do this 'for' other people or in other people's spaces. You can share the tools and the wisdom—however, allow others to implement the process for themselves.

Why didn't we talk about zero?

Your address may have a 0 in it, but the numerology will not sum up to 0. Therefore, having a home with a 0 energy environment is out of the cards. Your personal numerology will not sum up to a 0 either.

When we look at the 0, it's like a quartz crystal: it magnifies or amplifies whatever number it's connected to. Similarly, the 0 has no character traits or personality attributes other than to enhance whatever it's connected to.

For example, the number 10 reduces to 1 (independence), thus if you wanted to look at the characteristics of the 10, it would be the independent nature of the 1 kicked up a notch or even "optimized."

Should my address numerology match my personal numerology?

As a rule of thumb, I don't necessarily think it is effective to have the same Life Path number as your home. You certainly can do this! However, when you have a number as your foundational vibration, it already comes with your blueprint. When you choose to match that number with your environment, it can get really intense. This is not to say that if you you are a 3 Life Path—and are wanting to tap into creativity or open up your home for entertaining—that you cannot change your address numerology to a 3. Do it. Just be aware that you are magnifying your vibration. This means that you are magnifying the challenging traits along with the good ones.

It's similar with your Attitude number. Still very telling and relevant, the Attitude number makes a smaller impact on your blueprint, but the effect of this number may be diminished even further if you try to adjust all of your numbers to match it.

There are many facets to your life, and you can use different numbers to bring in more abundance in different ways and in different areas. Overall, the idea is to decide what kind of energy you want to generate in an environment and bring it into alignment with your desires, goals, and dreams. You can always test something out—you aren't married to it! Play with these numbers and don't get overwhelmed with ensuring that your personal numerology is a match to what you want to create.

Think of it this way: You are creating your own code between your address numerology and your personal numerology. Consider going for a well-rounded code that includes more of what you want to be instead of limiting yourself.

1	2	3	4	5	6	7	8	9
A	B	C	D	E	F	G	H	I
J	K	L	M	N	O	P	Q	R
S	T	U	V	W	X	Y	Z	

Can you calculate and use the numerology of the street name?

Of course you can, and I do! Everything is energy and has a vibration or frequency, thus has an associated number.

Use the Pythagorean alphabet numerology chart to calculate the street name.

For example:

2350 Sunny Lane

2+ 3 + 5 + 0 = 10, which equals 1

Next: Add up the the street name (do not add the numbers to the name—do them separately).

S = 1 U = 3 N = 5 N = 5 Y = 7

Add up Sunny [1+3+5+5+7] = 21

2 + 1 = 3

L = 3 A = 1 N = 5 E = 5

Add up Lane = 14

1 + 4 = 5

Add 3 + 5 = 8

Sunny Lane = 8

So, the address numerology is 1 and the street name numerology is 8. The 1 is the main energy—leadership, independence, self-sufficiency. The 8 is representative of the "area"—powerful ambitions, building momentum. If you look at the relationship between the 1 and the 8, both have qualities of leadership, drive, and success. Cool combo, but watch out for ego and greed. Read more on this in the next question.

What does the numerology of the street name mean?

The numerical portion (and apartment/unit number if applicable) is the main vibe and the easiest one to experiment with for results. The street/lane/avenue name of the location is not the predominant energy of the location. This is because the vibration of the street name is shared by many—thus, it is more representative of the "area" versus your specific space. I like to calculate both parts of the address numerology, however it is more challenging to recognize the effects of the actual street name because it is more subtle. So, I encourage you to play with the numerical portion of your address first and see what unfolds.

Knowing the vibration of your street name will help you

understand an added dimension of the personality of the address, however it is not necessary nor is it commonly factored into the immediate numerology. If you really get into this, you can calculate the city, state, county, and zip code. It's quite interesting, but don't get bogged down in these details. Stick to the basics of the numerical portion of the address you are analyzing in order to realize the most profound effects and shifts. This is where you get the biggest bang for your buck and influence the most change in your energetic field. Less is more.

What about the Abundance Code of my...

Driver License?
Social Security Number?
Passport Number?
P.O. Box?

I think you are starting to get the idea that the Abundance Codes are everywhere! Once you start seeing numbers and thinking about how they relate to you, that's where YOU gain empowerment to shift the energies to create what YOU want to experience in YOUR life.

Driver License or Identification Card:

Yes, your driver license does have an energy to it. Add up the number on your driver license (DL) or identification card and come up with its numerology.

What does it mean? Think of your DL or ID as a part of your "identity." Once you add up the numbers and find the numerology, ask yourself the following:

How does this number's energy relate to my identity? Is there a pattern?

Is there anything associated with this number and its lower traits that I want to work on? If so, this will help you think about how you may be getting in your own way.

For example:

Say your driver license or ID is 02256360

$0 + 2 + 2 + 5 + 6 + 3 + 6 + 0 = 24$

$2 + 4 = 6$

6, as we know, offers the energy of the nurturer and the caregiver. The 6 contains compassionate vibrations and taps into the feeling of unconditional love. In detriment, the 6 vibration can also create an environment where you put others ahead of yourself rather than focusing on "self-care."

With the above example of a 6 driver license, you might consider your identity and how other people perceive you when asking these questions:

Where can I practice more compassion toward myself and others?
Am I nurturing to others, and myself, mutually?
Do I make adequate time for myself?
Do I express my feelings honestly to myself and those around me?
Do I have people-pleasing tendencies that I could work through to find more empowerment?

If you feel like the 6 is effectively working in your life, great! If not, you can change this too. Follow the instructions for changing the numerology of your car. Determine what energy you want to incorporate into your identity. Like the other examples, you will figure out the number you need to add to the number you have in order to get the number you want. Write the "number you need" out on a tiny piece of paper. Tape it on the back of your DL or ID.

Caution: Be mindful here. Your DL or ID is a legal document, so don't deface it. Make something that is easily removable.

Social Security Number, National Identification Number, Etc.

The social security card has an energy too. Just like before, you add the numbers up to come up with the numerology. However, I don't suggest changing the numerology of your social security card. This is a number that never changes as it relates to your country of citizenship, so it says something about the energy of your identification. This number is assigned to you for identification and usually tax purposes for the country of your citizenship.

Things to think about: What does this number say about me as a citizen of this country?

Do I live out the positive associated number values/ energies in my daily life as relates to my country?

Passport Number:

The passport number is fun to look at. Think of it as part of your international identity. Our passport numbers change when we renew them, and they are usually valid for 10 years (this can vary). I would not suggest changing your passport numerology. Rather, I would consider what energies it is evoking in your life and in your travels.

Ask yourself: How can I harness the energy of the (fill in the blank with the number) in order to create and enrich my experiences? When I travel, am I using positive aspects of (fill in the number) to optimize these energies? Are there any 'bad behaviors' associated with this number that I could learn from while traveling?
 Don't forget to take into account the low vibes or challenging characteristics of the number and see how they might be limiting you when you travel. Check out the intentions associated with each number in Chapter 4 for ideas on clearing blocks and creating breakthroughs with any of the limited or outdated belief systems associated with that number which you may be

harboring.

You could also look at a Visa or Residency Card as a "temporary" international identification number and consider these questions: What does this reflect on my identification/identity at this time in my life? Am I tapping into the highest vibrations and abundance of this energy?

Set intentions around the travel element in your life, reason for travel, and energy of the number to maximize a more abundant experience.

P.O. Box:

You don't live in this box, so it isn't affecting the energy of your environment. It is simply a placeholder for your mail. This number doesn't have a hefty bearing on your identity or environment. I wouldn't suggest changing it— the Post Office might get (appropriately) huffy. And it may uncharitably confuse the mail handler (wink!)

You can certainly do the numerology of the P.O. Box for fun. Just use the numbers. There is no need to factor in the alphabet of the "P.O."

The energy of your P.O Box is just another cool thing to examine. If you're nerding out on this, then I'm thrilled that you are noticing that number codes are everywhere.

What about the energy of my garden?

Your garden is another wonderful opportunity to use numerology to tap into abundance. If you have a garden at your home or adjoining property, you can change the numerology of that piece/section of the property to reflect the energy you want to create in your garden.

You will use the same base number from your address numerology to start. The cool thing is that you can change the numerology of the inside of your home, and you can change the numerology of the garden, separately, using the same base number from your address. This is because they are locked into the same code, but in two separate spaces or specified environments.

1. Determine the numerology of your home address.

2. Decide what you want your garden to reflect. You might want to consider a 2 for balance and harmony among the plants, or a 3 for creativity and new growth, or

a 6 for love and nurturing, or an 8 for general abundance. It's up to you! Ask the plants what they want and trust your first impression and intuition on the response they give you.

3. Determine what "number you need" to add to the base number of your address in order to equal the number/energy you want. [Reminder: Do not simply write the number you're wanting. This will not work, and you will affect the numerology in a completely different way than you are intending.]

4. Write the number down on something waterproof (laminate the paper, get a number sticker, etc.). Get creative. It can even be a fun, decorative number.

5. Put the "number you need" on a small stake. Stick it in a strategic or intuitive place in your garden. I would suggest one of the four corners, if applicable.

This will not affect the energy of your home because it is intended specifically for the energy of your garden or designated area in a yard.

Reminder: When calculating and changing the numerology of your garden, use your original address numerology to find the "number you need," not the number you might have posted inside the house, and not the ideal number you are seeking.

Can I change the Abundance Code in a specific room in my house?

Yes, you could alter the numerology of a specific room, but I do not recommend this unless you are really savvy and comfortable with numerology. You could determine the number you want to call into a specific room and place the number that you need to get you to that specific vibration inside the door.

Again, this is something I don't do nor do I suggest doing it. Why? If I choose an energy for my home or home-office space (even if they are one in the same—which, for me, they actually are), I commit to the vibrations of that number and set intentions associated with the number for and around my personal life and professional life in that shared space.

Can I change the Abundance Code in my hotel room?

Absolutely, and I do, all the time! For example, if I end up in a hotel room that adds up to a 5, I change it. Here's what you want to do: Calculate the address numerology of the hotel and add in the room number to get the numerology of the room. If you decide to change it, follow the basic instructions by determining the number you want for that hotel room, figure out the number you need to get it, write the "number you need" on a post-it, and then stick it inside the door for the night or for the duration of your stay. Voila!

Can I change the Abundance Code of my cubicle or office space at a large office?

YES! I would totally do this because it will make a difference and can positively impact the quality of your work and mindset in that environment. Determine the address numerology of your office. Once you've done this, follow all the instructions for changing the address. Write the "number you need" to get the number you want on a post-it and stick it just inside the cubicle or inside the door of your office.

How often can I change the numerology of my spaces?

Commit to the new number for at least 6-8 months. Be patient: allow the energies to take effect and shift. This is how you will experience the most effective and lasting results. I promise!

Final Thoughts

This isn't solely about changing the energy of your environment—it's about evoking and realizing a change in yourself that is in alignment with what you want to transform in your life. It's about choosing to collaborate with your destiny.

When you intentionally recognize ("re-cognize:" to cognitively reprocess) what limitations you have constructed (real or imagined) from previous experiences, your energy has already shifted. You have already reconditioned your energetic space to make room for something new to come in. The Abundance Codes are about tapping into something greater, wiser, and more expansive than what currently exists for you.

By playing with the energy of your environment, identifying the limitations, determining what you want to manifest or call into your reality, finding a number that will help you do so in your physical environment, and then trusting the process... the pieces of your cosmic puzzle magically and effortlessly begin to fall together into a new pattern for your life.

And your life takes off in the direction of your dreams. Bon voyage!

Amanda Rieger Green, MPH

Amanda combines her psychic gifts with her life experience—a soul journey through trauma, addiction, and depression—to guide clients in understanding their own unique life blueprint and innate abilities in order to align with their soul mission.

She is the founder of Soul Pathology, a life practice designed to reconnect our

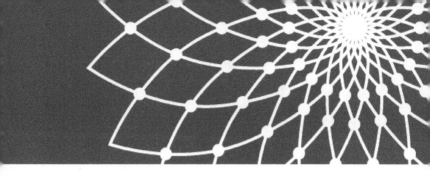

human and spirit selves, heal soul-defragmentation, and illuminate our soul path. She also is a co-founder of Wise Skies Advice, an astrology and numerology business that offers tools, resources and products for people who want to tap into the magic of good timing.

Amanda is a graduate of Sewanee, The University of the South, with a B.A. in Religion. Additionally, she holds a Master of Public Health from Boston University. She is a certified yoga instructor and Reconnective Healing practitioner. Amanda is blissfully (yes, blissfully) married to Dennis Green. They split their time between Austin, Texas and Belize with their two Labrador Retrievers, Tex & Ouisie (short for Texas & Louisiana).

CPSIA information can be obtained
at www.ICGtesting.com
Printed in the USA
FSHW011625181118
53820FS

9 780997 734973